FRESHWATER FEEDERS

Studying Food Webs in Freshwater

GWENDOLYN HOOKS

Rourke
Publishing LLC

Vero Beach, FL 32964
rourkepublishing.com

www.rourkepublishing.com

Project Assistance:
Also, the author thanks Darleen Bailey Beard, Dr. Edmond Hooks, Julie K. Lundgren, Jane McKellips and the team at Blue Door Publishing.

Photo credits: Cover Images - Lily Pads © Stephanie Connell, Little Blue Heron © Bob Blanchard, Frog © Cynthia Kidwell, Water Snail © Rustam Burganov, Algae © Darla Hallmark; Page 4 © Arid Ocean, Cherick; Page 6 © SueC, Peter Baxter; Page 7 © Don Mace; Page 8 © Karl Havens; Page 9 © USGS, Galyna Andrushko, Dr. Ralf Wagner, Karl Havens, eb33 Page 10 © Andrzej Gibasiewicz, Peter Baxter; Page 11 © Teze; Page 12 © iofoto; Page 13 © Elena Elisseeva; Page 14 © Veledan; Page 15 © Stephen Girimont, Anna; Page 16 © Darla Hallmark, Karl Havens, Cynthia Kidwell, Galyna Andrushko, Bryan Faust; Page 18 © Jeff Delonge, Evanherk; Page 19 © Steve McWilliam; Page 21 © Jiri Vaclavek, Adenosine; Page 23 © M Willis, Cherick; Page 24 © Jake Hellbach; Page 25 © Lilac Mountain; Page 27 © westphalia; Page 28 © Phinfish, Bryan Faust, Page 29 © Matt Edmonds

Editor: Jeanne Sturm

Cover and page design by Nicola Stratford, Blue Door Publishing

Library of Congress Cataloging-in-Publication Data

Hooks, Gwendolyn.
   Freshwater feeders : studying food webs in freshwater / Gwendolyn Hooks.
      p. cm. -- (Studying food webs)
   Includes index.
   ISBN 978-1-60472-317-5 (hardcover)
   ISBN 978-1-60472-782-1 (softcover)
   1. Freshwater ecology--Juvenile literature. 2. Food chains
(Ecology)--Juvenile literature. I. Title.
   QH541.5.F7H66 2009
   577.6'16--dc22

Printed in the USA

CG/CG

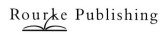

Rourke Publishing
www.rourkepublishing.com – rourke@rourkepublishing.com
Post Office Box 3328, Vero Beach, FL 32964

Table Of Contents

Rivers, Lakes, Ponds, and Streams   4

Dining in an Underwater World   12

In and Out of Food Webs   17

Breaking Down and Building Up   20

Unlinked!   22

Glossary   30

Index   32

On The Cover

Little Blue Herons prey on frogs and fish.

Most frogs eat insects, snails, and worms.

Water snails nibble on algae and other aquatic plants.

Algae produces energy when zapped by sunlight.

Rivers, Lakes, Ponds, and Streams

Earth's surface is more than 70 percent water, but only 1 percent is freshwater. Freshwater contains very little salt. Lakes, ponds, rivers, and streams are freshwater resources. Besides drinking water, they provide water for sanitation, industry, agriculture, recreation, and food.

Lakes are large bodies of water surrounded by land. Ponds are smaller. Rivers and streams have flowing water. Each type of freshwater has its own **ecosystem**. An ecosystem is made up of plants and animals and non-living things such as water and **nutrients**. The most important part of any ecosystem is its energy source, usually the Sun.

U N I T E D

CHEW ON THIS

Scientists often study small samples of water so they can better understand how ecosystems work in nature.

Lake Superior

Lake Huron

Lake Michigan

Lake Ontario

Lake Erie

The Great Lakes (Huron, Ontario, Michigan, Erie, and Superior) contain almost 20 percent of the world's freshwater supply. Lake Michigan is the only Great Lake located completely within the United States.

S T A T E S

Some freshwater animals feed on phytoplankton. Phytoplankton are tiny free-floating plants and plant-like organisms. Algae are phytoplankton, but are not true plants since they do not have roots, stems, and leaves.

Both phytoplankton and plants produce energy when zapped by sunlight. This process is called photosynthesis. Phytoplankton and plants are **primary producers**. They are the only organisms to make their own food.

Salmon have adapted to swim upstream to spawn or lay eggs.

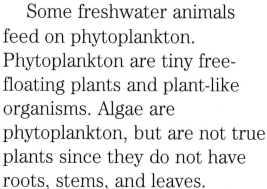

CHEW ON THIS

More marine biologists study phytoplankton and zoo-plankton than study whales.

A crowd of kokanee salmon make their way upstream in a northern California waterway.

Small animals called zooplankton feed on phytoplankton. Zooplankton are **primary consumers**. As they feed on phytoplankton, zooplankton absorb the energy they need to grow.

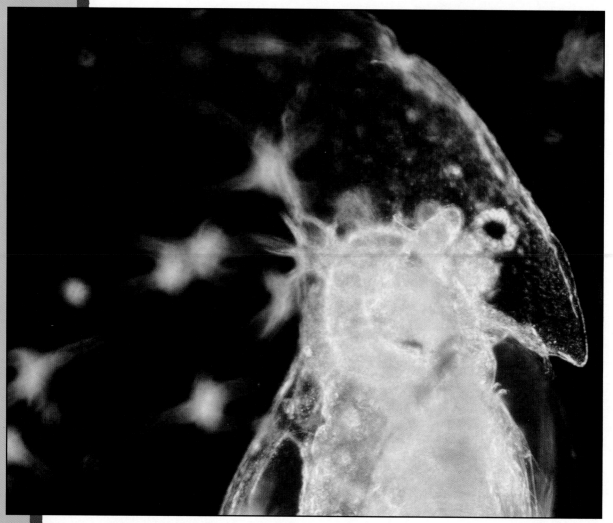

Daphnia retrocurva is a zooplankton found in lakes. Scientists believe its clear helmet conceals its body size from predators. This photograph shows what it looks like under a microscope.

The Sun, phytoplankton, zooplankton, and other plants and animals are linked together. The first link connects the Sun and phytoplankton. Zooplankton feeding upon phytoplankton forms another link. Small fish eat zooplankton and larger fish eat the smaller fish. These connected links are called a **food chain**.

Freshwater jellyfish prefer farm ponds. Some are the size of a penny. They are almost transparent with a hint of white or green tint. Like ocean jellyfish, they have tentacles to sting tasty zooplankton before gobbling them up.

A Freshwater Food Chain

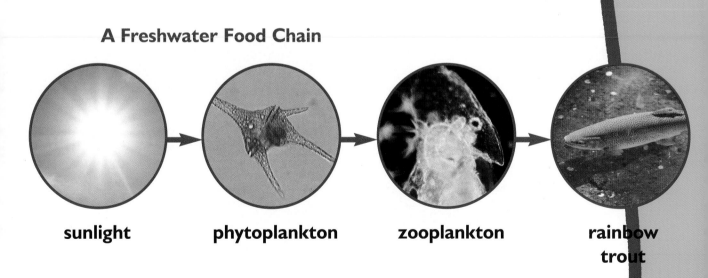

sunlight   phytoplankton   zooplankton   rainbow trout

Patterson Elementary School
3731 Lawrence Drive
Naperville, IL 60564

Food links are more complex than they appear because many animals eat more than one type of food. Some eat zooplankton when they are young, but insects when they become adults. Others eat both zooplankton and insects throughout their lives. When food chains in ecosystems overlap and interconnect, they become **food webs**.

Some fish move from one ecosystem to another. Atlantic salmon may spend up to six years in rivers feeding on insects and fish. Then they swim into the Atlantic Ocean where they change their diets to include squid, shrimp, and fish. At spawning time, they return to the river of their birth, changing diets once again.

Crater Lake, in Oregon, is home to kokanee salmon and rainbow trout. Kokanee salmon eat squishy zooplankton while rainbow trout dine on chewy insects.

CHEW ON THIS

Ecologists study how organisms interact with the other plants and animals in their environment.

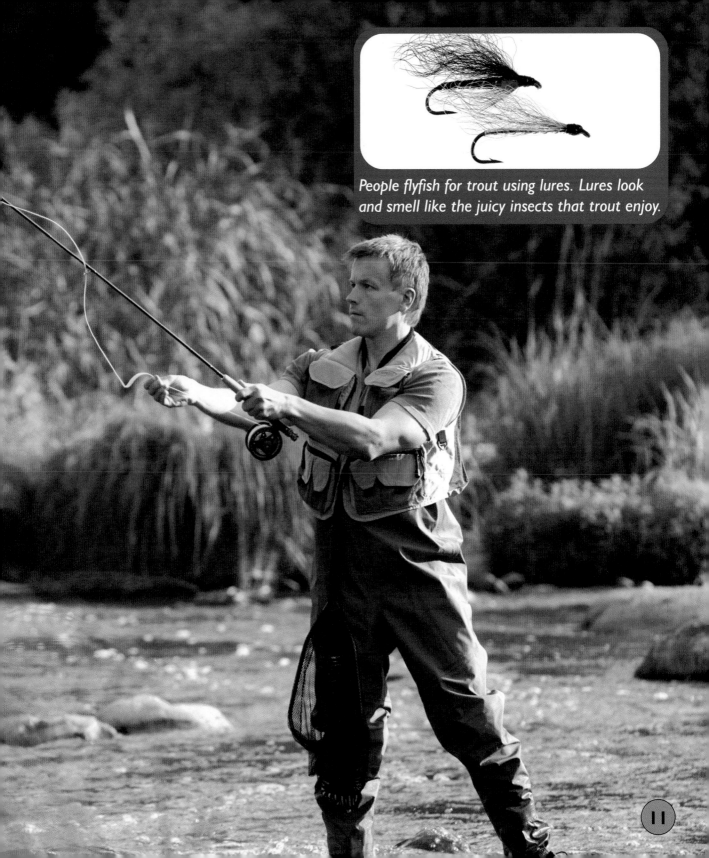

People flyfish for trout using lures. Lures look and smell like the juicy insects that trout enjoy.

Dining in an Underwater World

Whether river, stream, lake, or pond, each source of freshwater hosts a wealth of feeding activity. Some plants and animals prefer the swift currents of a river, while others like the slow pace of lakes and ponds. Caddis fly **larvae** and mayfly nymphs have adapted to swift flowing rivers by clinging to rocky bottoms. Species like trout, smallmouth bass, and walleye feed on insects and minnows that swarm in fast moving rivers and streams. Plants in these swift waters need a strong root system to survive, unlike slow-water plants that may even be free floating.

The Mississippi River flows from Lake Itasca in Minnesota to its mouth in the Gulf of Mexico. It is 2,302 miles (3,705 kilometers) long.

The Mississippi River provides habitats for:

- 241 species of fish
- 37 species of mussels
- 45 species of amphibians
- 50 species of mammals
- 40 percent of migrating birds

in the United States.

Still waters allow plants to grow easily. The plants are not strongly rooted and tend to grow near shores. They provide food and a habitat for amphibians, fish, and waterfowl. Bottom dwelling insects include midges and sludge worms. Fish such as carp prefer still waters and get their food from the debris on the bottom of ponds.

Wetlands

Marshes, swamps, and bogs are types of wetlands. Water covers some wetlands part of the year. Other wetlands are covered in water all year long. Flowers, grasses, and bushes grow in marshes. Swamps are slow moving rivers filled with trees and shrubs. Bogs contain shrubs, evergreens, and mosses.

Wetlands serve an important role in ecosystems. The plant matter they release into rivers provides food for fish. Migratory birds use wetlands as resting places during their long journeys and as places to feed.

Bladderworts are actually plants that eat tiny insects and fish. Through their bladder-like trap, they suck up their prey and devour it for much needed nutrients.

Water lilies grow in ponds or lakes. The Giant Water Lily, found in the Amazon River, grows up to 6 feet (1.8 m) across.

Animals that graze on plants and phytoplankton are **herbivores**. Herbivores are primary consumers. Animals that eat other animals are **carnivores**. Carnivores are **secondary consumers**. **Omnivores** eat both plants and phytoplankton, and they also eat other animals. Omnivores are secondary consumers.

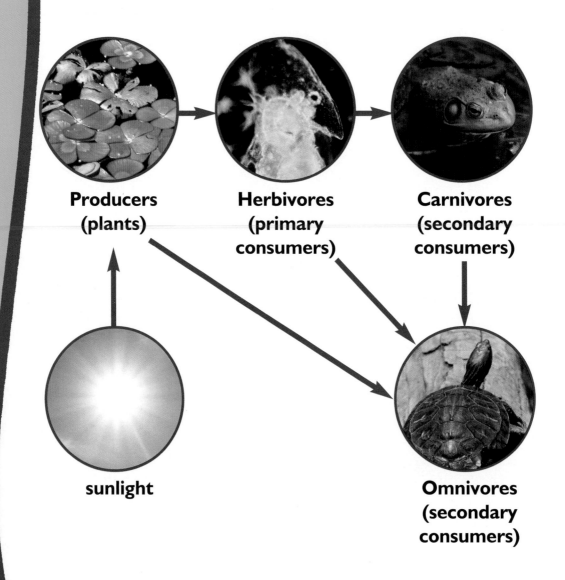

Producers (plants)

Herbivores (primary consumers)

Carnivores (secondary consumers)

sunlight

Omnivores (secondary consumers)

In and Out of Food Webs

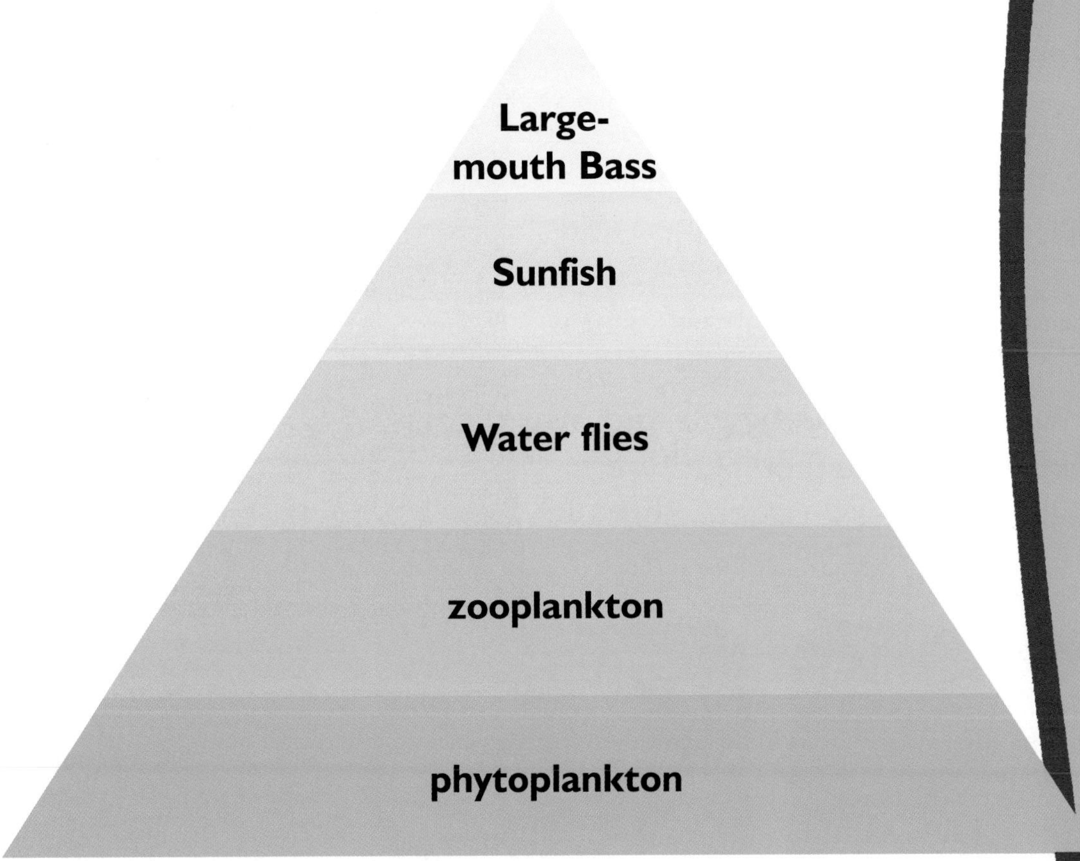

Large-mouth Bass

Sunfish

Water flies

zooplankton

phytoplankton

Scientists can classify plants and animals by their trophic or nutrimental level. The bottom of the trophic triangle is larger than the step above it because more phytoplankton and aquatic plants exist than zooplankton. From one level to the next, about 90 percent of the available energy is lost. Energy is also lost as animals move about to capture food.

Even animals like snails that do not chase and capture food must use energy. They travel toward food and graze on plant matter the same way that a deer munches on grass. Clams and mussels are filter feeders. They suck water inside their shells and over their gills. After the food is filtered through, the excess water is shot out.

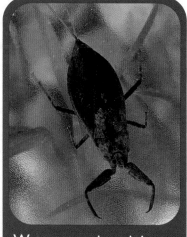

Water scorpions inject their prey with saliva, turning it into a soupy shake.

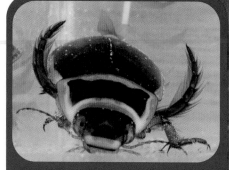

The predaceous diving beetle is a **predator** that chases its **prey**. It grabs insects, tadpoles, and other diving beetles with its pinchers and crushes them with its powerful jaws.

Ramshorn snails graze on the algae that coat water plants.

Breaking Down and Building Up

Eventually, everything must die, even predators at the top of the food chain. The bodies of dead animals and plants are broken down by **decomposers**. Decomposers eat dead things to get energy.

Decomposers, like bacteria, rely on scavengers to first tear the plants and animals into small pieces as they feed. Then the decomposers take over the job. Decomposers are recyclers. As they feed on dead matter and turn it into nutrients, the nutrients are released into the water.

Tadpoles eat decayed or rotted aquatic plants.

Unlinked!

Pollution occurs when a contaminant has been released into freshwater. A contaminant is anything that alters the natural environment. It's usually the result of human activity. Pollution can make extinct, or totally wipe out, diverse species of plants and animals.

CHEW ON THIS

The Topeka shiner is listed as a threatened species. Scientists believe the introduction of predator fish like bass and northern pike is one cause for the shiner's decrease in numbers.

Conservation biologists work to maintain a natural balance between freshwater ecosystems and people's need for food, water, shelter, and recreation.

ENVIRONMENT IN DANGER!

Chemicals, heat, and organic waste are some of the causes of pollution in freshwater. Currents in rivers and streams can wash away chemical pollutants. Lakes, ponds, and wetlands can't cope as well because without currents they don't have the ability to wash away chemicals. Instead, the pollutants must be removed by humans or broken down by bacteria.

Plants and animals suffer when their habitat is damaged.

Sometimes industries dump waste water into freshwater. Often, this waste water is a different temperature than the water into which it is being dumped. This new temperature causes stress to plants and animals that live in the environment. Waste water also contains substances that are not native to the water system, changing the established ecosystem.

CHEW ON THIS

Climate change affects water supplies. Melting glaciers add more water to the world's rivers. This causes the water levels to rise.

Sometimes scientists identify healthy water by the species present. If stonefly larvae and mayfly larvae are absent, then there may be a problem with the water.

All living things, people, animals, and plants, need water to live. So it's up to people to protect freshwater from pollutants and to keep food webs from becoming unlinked.

Adult stonefly

Stonefly larvae live under-water in fast moving, clear streams. Fish, birds, spiders, and other insects feed on them.

Mayfly larvae live underwater for several years. Adults live only a day or two, just long enough to mate.

Glossary

carnivores (KAR-nuh-vorz): animals that eat other animals

decomposers (dee-cum-POH-zerz): animals and plants that cause rot and decay, enriching the soil with valuable nutrients

ecosystem (EE-koh-sis-tum): the relationships between all the plants and animals and the place in which they live

food chain (FOOD CHAYN): a series of plants and animals, each of which is eaten by the one after it

food web (FOOD WEHB): in an ecosystem, the intricate network of food chains

herbivores (hur-buh-vorz): animals that feed on plants and phytoplankton

larvae (lar-vuh): plural for larva, the young form of an animal

nutrients (NOO-tree-uhnts): the substances that plants and animals need to grow

omnivores (AHM-nih-vorz): animals that feed on a wide variety of foods including both plants and animals

pollution (puh-LOO-shuhn): to change the natural levels of plants and animals destroying them in the process

predator (PRED-uh-tur): animals that hunt other animals for food

prey (pray): animals that are hunted and eaten by other animals

primary consumers (PRYE-mair-ee kahn-SOO-merz): herbivores, the animals that eat primary producers

primary producers (PRYE-mair-ee proh-DOO-serz): plants that perform photosynthesis

secondary consumers (SEK-uhn-der-ee kuhn-SOO-murz): animals that eat herbivores

Further Reading

Want to learn more about freshwater food webs? The following books and websites are a great place to start.

Books

Barnes, Julia. *101 Facts about Lakes*. Gareth Stevens Publishing, 2004.

Davis, Barbara J. *Biomes and Ecosystems.*
    Gareth Stevens Publishing, 2007.

Johnson, Rebecca. *Journey into a Lake*. Carolrhoda Books, 2004.

Websites

Lakes Are Great

http://www.dnr.state.wi.us/org/caer/ce/eek/nature/habitat/lakes.htm

Rivers and Streams

http://www.mbgnet.net/fresh/rivers/index.htm

Ponds and Lakes

http://www.mbgnet.net/fresh/lakes/index.htm

Wetlands

http://www.mbgnet.net/fresh/wetlands/index.htm

Index

algae   6, 19
carnivores   16
ecosystem   4, 10, 23, 26
filter feeders   18
food chains   10
food webs   10, 17
herbivores   16
nutrients   4, 14, 20
omnivores   16
phytoplankton   6, 8, 9, 16, 17

pollution   21, 25
predators   8, 20
prey   14, 18
primary consumers   8, 16
primary producers   6
secondary consumers   16
wetlands   14, 25

About the Author

Gwendolyn Hooks has been an avid reader all of her life. When she was a child and supposed to be asleep, Gwendolyn sat by her window and used the streetlight to read "just one more chapter." Gwendolyn graduated from the University of Missouri-St. Louis with an education degree. Still an avid reader, she now writes fiction and nonfiction for children. This is her seventh book for young readers. She has three adult children and lives in Oklahoma City with her husband.